The Ghost of
Berry Pomeroy
Castle

Deryck Seymour

*"There are more things in heaven and earth, Horatio, than are
dreamt of in your philosophy."*
Hamlet, Act I, Scene v

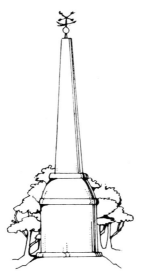

OBELISK PUBLICATIONS

ALSO BY THE AUTHOR
The Ghosts of Torbay
The Magic Triangle–South of the Teign Estuary
The Secret Circle–Ashburton to Newton Abbot to Totnes
Dart Country–Stoke Gabriel, Churston, Kingswear, Galmpton

OTHER TITLES IN THIS SERIES
The Ghosts of Exeter, *Sally and Chips Barber*
The Ghosts of Brixham, *Graham Wyley*
The Ghosts of Totnes, *Bob Mann*
The Ghosts of Plymouth, *Nancy Hammonds*
Dark and Dastardly Dartmoor, *Sally and Chips Barber*
Ghastly and Ghostly Devon, *Sally and Chips Barber*
Weird and Wonderful Dartmoor, *Sally and Chips Barber*
Haunted Pubs in Devon, *Sally and Chips Barber*
Haunted Happenings in Devon, *Judy Chard*
Murders and Mysteries in Devon, *Ann James*

OTHER OBELISK PUBLICATIONS ABOUT THIS AREA
The Great Little Totnes Book, *Chips Barber with Bill Bennett*
The Totnes Collection, *Bill Bennett*
Boat Trip Down the Dart, *Bob Mann*
Torbay in Colour–Torquay, Paignton, Brixham, *Chips Barber*
*We have over 140 Devon titles – for full list please send an s.a.e. to Obelisk Publications
at 2 Church Hill, Pinhoe, Exeter, Devon, EX4 9ER, or telephone Exeter (01392) 468556*

This book is dedicated with many good wishes to Jack and Joan Hazzard.

ACKNOWLEDGEMENTS
My thanks to the following people: Mrs Ali Khan, Mr C. Barber, Mr F. J. Bodley, Mrs A. Broughton, Mr Bullocke, Mr Bridgeman, Mrs Brighouse, Miss E. Beveridge, Mr R. Daulby, Mr A. Ellis, Mrs R. Everitt, Mrs M. Hartshorn, the late Mrs D. Hopwood, Mr W. Hunt, Mr J. Hazzard, Mrs S. Joint, Mrs E. Jerrard, Mr P. Kird, Mrs May, Mr Moore, Mrs H. Phillips, Mr D.W. Roddy, Mrs Rowden, Mr Craig Rowland, Miss H. Reilly, Miss R. Ramsden, Mrs A. Wright and Mr L. J. Sawyer.

PLATE ACKNOWLEDGEMENTS:
Jane Reynolds for pages 11, 13, 15, 17 and 22, and for the cover drawings
Mr Bridgeman for page 16 and Aerofilms Ltd for page 24
Sally and Chips Barber for all other photographs

*First published in 1990, Reprinted in 1992, 1994 and 1996
by Obelisk Publications, 2 Church Hill, Pinhoe, Exeter, Devon,
Designed by Chips and Sally Barber
Edited and Typeset by Sally Barber
Printed in Great Britain*

© Deryck Seymour/Obelisk Publications
All Rights Reserved. No part of this publication may be reproduced, stored in a retrieval system, or transmitted, in any form or by any means, electronic, mechanical, photocopying, recording or otherwise, without the prior permission of the publishers and copyright holders.

The Ghosts of Berry Pomeroy Castle

Introduction

Ghosts! A spine-chilling subject for a book, you must admit, but the booksellers told me that everyone is interested in ghosts. 'Do write us a book on ghosts,' they said. Well, here it is! It concerns Berry Pomeroy Castle and is a collection of psychic experiences which people I know had at or near the castle. Stories related at second hand always lack the ring of authenticity for the very simple reason that you cannot question the person who was actually concerned. These experiences were all given to me by reliable witnesses. The ramblings of over-credulous and whimsical folk have been rigorously excluded. With regard to the title of this book I have used the word "ghost" in its loosest possible sense. Most of the stories related here are not to do with visible ghosts, but rather to ghostly occurrences which can more correctly, perhaps, be termed "psychic phenomena"—a splendid all-embracing term, but not perhaps such a good title for a book.

The question now arises as to whether I, the author, believe in ghosts. Could I be just writing about them and no more? Well, my nature is sensitive, but I would not describe myself as psychic. Nevertheless, I have seen what I can only believe to have been a ghost face to face, one bright September afternoon—not at Berry but at Upton Parish Church, Torquay, when a charming little old lady passed right beside me in the porch, opened the door to enter the church only to vanish from view immediately. What, I wonder, would I have felt if I had tried to shake hands with her? We half smiled at each other by way of greeting, so she evidently saw me. Fortunately a friend of mine who had just left the church saw her too—a few seconds before I did. He saw her walk into the porch and described her exactly as I had seen her. Yet she had vanished and was nowhere to be seen in the building. For me this was proof positive of the existence of psychic phenomena.

As to what a ghost really is—that is a scientific matter far beyond my ken. With regard to some apparitions and sounds, I am inclined to think that these may be no more than impressions on the atmosphere and are akin to tapes and records which, under certain circumstances, may go on repeating. But far more sinister and in quite a different category are the evil forces which from time to time make themselves felt at Berry. There is the feeling of unreasonable fear, that sudden physical disability, the going back in time, shadows and aromas—none of these can be dismissed as mere impressions on the atmosphere. They are phenomena far more unpleasant which can impress themselves on

receptive individuals at any moment in time and completely upset their mental poise. The usual result with such visitors is that they leave the castle as quickly as possible, resolving never to go there again. I know many who have been affected thus. What the potent force may be which produces this kind of reaction is, as it were, the hard core of my subject. It is this power which interests me so much.

The reader should be careful to distinguish between the psychic experiences related in this book and the ghost story of fiction. All the occurrences now to be related really were experienced by those who recounted them to me. The possibility that any of them were spinning a yarn or exaggerating what was at best a figment of the imagination is most remote. All are people of sense and integrity, and I ask the reader to accept this fact. I have been able to record no less than 14 different kinds of phenomena at or around the castle, but there is one kind which so far has not been reported, and that is the appearance at close hand of a being so closely resembling flesh and blood that their sudden disappearance comes as a real shock.

After reading this book many more are sure to join the ranks of ghost hunters; indeed some new to the game may set out this very night in the hope of seeing something. Although as a rule all is quiet and peaceful, yet much has been seen and felt at Berry over the years, so you may be lucky! But here a word of caution. The buildings and woods are dangerous to explore at night—especially if you are alone. I am always apprehensive of reading that someone has been found injured through falling. A stumble on those precipitous crags on which the castle is so ingeniously perched could be nasty by day, but by night it could be fatal. Always tell someone if you decide to go alone to Berry, and if you are going to do a prolonged watch then see that you are warmly clad and have plenty of food with you. If you are both cold and hungry then your senses of perception will be much impaired. If fear should suddenly strike you, then don't be ashamed to mention it to your companions, they may be just as scared as yourself! If you are deeply afraid, then go home whilst the going is good. This applies particularly if you are alone. You will read further on how fear at this castle seems to build up until a state of near panic is reached. Then it is that the evil power which seems to lurk at Berry may confront you. And this is a thing to be avoided at all costs. Should you have a psychic experience then do please report it to me. If everyone had done that over the past ten years then I am certain that this book would have been twice the length. So much may yet be learnt from the Berry Pomeroy hauntings that it is a pity for one experience to go unrecorded. After all, is it not said to be the most haunted castle in England?

A Brief History of Berry Pomeroy Castle

At this point a short account of the castle's history will not come amiss. For a more detailed account the reader is referred to my previous book *Berry Pomeroy Castle*. The manor of Beri belonged at the time of the Norman Conquest to Alric—a rich Saxon thegn—who owned several manors in this part of the country. He was dispossessed by William the Conqueror, and this particular manor was bestowed upon Ralf de la Pomerai as a reward for services rendered at the time of the battle of Hastings. His family stronghold in Normandy was the Chateau Ganne whose ruins still stand near Caen, and are situated close to the village of La Pomeraye from which the family derived its name. There were nineteen generations of de la Pomerais (Pomeroy being the later spelling of the name) and they held the castle and manor until 1548, when Sir Thomas Pomeroy sold Berry and Bridgetown (Totnes) to Edward Seymour, brother to Queen Jane Seymour, who was the third wife of King Henry VIII. He became the first Duke of Somerset and

Lord Protector of the Realm when the boy King Edward VI succeeded to the throne in 1547. So at the time of the purchase of the castle he was the most powerful man in the land. However, he was soon to be toppled from power by his enemies, and after a summary trial was executed in 1552. His son, Lord Edward Seymour, managed to secure Berry, although through his father's second marriage he had been disinherited. It was apparently he and his son, Sir Edward Seymour, who lavished vast sums of money on a palatial new wing. But the time of the Seymours at Berry was to be tragically short, for after the death of the third Baronet in 1688 no other member of the family ever lived there. The castle became deserted, largely because the fourth Baronet's interests lay entirely in London where he was for many years Speaker of the House of Commons. By about 1800 the building was completely deserted. The Seymour family have never parted with Berry, however, and the castle belongs today to the 19th Duke of Somerset. Under a Deed of Guardianship (1977) the actual castle is maintained by English Heritage who succeeded the Ministry of the Environment. Much restoration work has been carried out during the past decade, and the walls which were becoming ruinous and dangerous have been made safe. It stands deserted and abandoned — the wreck of a stately building—a tragedy in broken stones. For nearly two centuries it has been left completely to its own devices— a haunt for bats and owls and all things sinister. Small wonder that the ghosts took over.

Collected Evidence of Psychic Phenomena

Everyone who has ever heard of Berry Pomeroy Castle seems also to have heard that it is haunted; yet very few who have been there will admit to having had a psychic experience. I can tell you, nevertheless, of over 80 living people who would at this moment be prepared to testify as to the truth of the strange things which happened to them at or near the castle. Some of these, surprisingly, are quite hardened sceptics. But in collecting these experiences I feel that there are very many more to be gleaned from those who are perhaps a little afraid of being laughed at, and so hold back data which would be so valuable in research of the kind which I am undertaking. I feel at times that I have only touched the tip of the iceberg

Certain deductions can be made from the study of these accounts when closely analysed. In the first place—perhaps surprisingly—the bulk of the activity has taken place in daylight hours, only one visible ghost—the White Lady appearing by night. This is surely odd when one considers that ghosts are notoriously nocturnal. Or is this, perhaps, a misapprehension which has been taken too much for granted? Could it not rather be that we ourselves are more tranquil and receptive when free from the stress of daylight activities? Sounds, of course will be more readily heard in the silence of the night, but the paranormal activities themselves may be just as vigorous by day as by night.

As soon as I began listing the various phenomena which have manifested themselves there, I found that for convenience sake they could be placed under separate categories. So far I can list 14 distinct phenomena which are as follows: (1) unreasonable fear, (2) visible appearances, (3) very cold air, usually accompanied by shivering and hair standing on end, (4) paranormal sounds, (5) being touched by an unseen person, (6) photographic failure i.e. blank films, cameras not working properly, shutters jamming etc, (7) engine failures at or near the castle, (8) failure of batteries, cars or floodlighting, (9) being taken over by another entity, (10) going back in time, (11) sudden physical disability, (12) appearance of shadows, (13) odours, (14) a power seems to emanate from the castle which can affect things and people far distant.

Many of the people now to be mentioned experienced more than one of these phenomena at the same time. Where this happened the individual will then be mentioned again under the appropriate heading.

1. Unreasonable Fear

This seems to be the commonest of all the phenomena experienced at the castle. Some visitors are so scared that they will not so much as enter the courtyard—their one idea being to get away as quickly as possible. Others will not even go down the drive. This feeling of fear may grip people quite suddenly. Mr Jack Hazzard, for some years foreman under the Ministry of the Environment, relates how visitors will suddenly leave when a moment before they were inspecting the buildings quite happily. He particularly recalls how a man went very white and then said that he was really too afraid to go any further; he departed as fast as his legs would carry him. Sometimes people feel that the buildings themselves are actually hostile. I have a good example of that in the case of Mrs Mary Hartshorn of Leigh-on-Sea who, with a Mr and Mrs Fore, visited the castle one night and wrote to me later as follows:

"When we reached the path leading to the Gatehouse we saw a faint, bluish-grey light coming from behind one of the windows, the one on the left as you face the Gatehouse: overhead was a small white cloud hovering over the building. All this time there was a feeling of malignant hostility, not so much from a person as from a force which was willing us to go away. I have never been so frightened, but being with a young couple, I felt I must fly the flag for my generation, and stand my ground, but I was thinking, 'I hope to God they don't want to go inside.' We then saw another fainter light below the window, and the young man's wife voiced the words that were running through my head, 'I don't like this, let's go'. The young man, though not admitting that he was afraid, raised no objection and the girl held his hand, telling me to do the same and clinging to each other we stumbled back to the car. We stopped at the same spot before we drove on, the light was still there, but the cloud had moved to the right, whence according to the young man it moved back again as though following us. I have lots of experience of haunted buildings with the Ghost Club, but have never felt such stark terror as I did that night."

The Ghosts of Berry Pomeroy Castle

Mrs Beryl Newman, a clergyman's widow, feels that great evil lurks at the castle and will not so much as enter the drive. She was much concerned for my well-being when she knew that I went frequently alone to Berry when preparing my book.

The late Mrs Dena Hopwood related to me how she visited the castle for the first time. It was just getting dusk on a summer's evening when she and her husband approached it from the valley below, always the most atmospheric approach. As soon as she entered the woods a feeling of great fear and oppression took hold of her; it was almost like a great weight on her head. On reaching the castle nothing would persuade her to pass through the gateway—her one instinct was to get away at all costs. Not until they got clear of the woods did she feel normal again.

Another friend of mine, Mrs Anne Wright, told me how she once visited the ruins with a Mrs Marion Smith. They were enjoying all they saw until they began to go along the Rampart Walk towards St. Margaret's Tower. Then they were both suddenly affected by an unreasonable fear and became cold and shivery. So frightened were they that they left as quickly as possible. Neither feel that they could ever make a return visit.

Mr R. Daulby, who is a member of the ASSAP and did much scientific research in connection with the hauntings, paid the castle a visit on a summer's evening in 1983 with a trainee medium who at first did not feel anything untoward, with the exception of St. Margaret's Tower which nothing would persuade her to enter. As twilight closed in she distinctly saw faces at some of the upstairs windows. As they prepared to leave they suddenly felt the presence of many spirits who wished them to be gone. In panic they scrambled over the gate, not waiting to unlock it. Neither felt that they could have gone back or that it would have been wise to do so. They simply did not feel it safe to stay another moment.

A Mrs Hilary Phillips who lives at Horrabridge, near Yelverton, related how she once visited the castle with her four children. She and her son Dominic, then aged twelve, descended the worn stairs to the dungeon in the southern tower of the Gatehouse. Here she suddenly became scared and felt as if bands had been placed round her head which were slowly being drawn tighter and ever tighter. She hastily grabbed Dominic and together they staggered up the narrow spiral stairs. On reaching the Guardroom she soon regained her composure, but noticed that her son was most upset. 'I didn't like it down there, mummy,' he said, and proceeded to describe almost the identical sensations which she had felt.

Mr D.W. Roddy of Torquay told me that as a young boy he and his brother visited the castle. They were quite happy exploring until they climbed down to the dungeon at the bottom of St. Margaret's Tower. Here they both became conscious of an unpleasant pressure on their temples and felt frightened and uncomfortable. So they evidently experienced similar sensations to Mrs Phillips and her son, but in a different dungeon. Several years after the first incident Mr Roddy visited Berry for a midnight picnic with several young friends. There was no moon and it was a pitch black night. At about 12.30 a.m. he and one of his friends saw a dim light traversing the top of the rampart wall (cf. Mrs Hartshorn's experience). It was very faint, more like a bluish haze. At the same time Mr Roddy experienced pressure on his temples. He was so frightened that he hurried to his car and drove off. He felt that there was something uncanny about the whole experience and has never paid another visit to the castle. He added that he would certainly never go there alone. His friend also saw the light but does not seem to have been so scared.

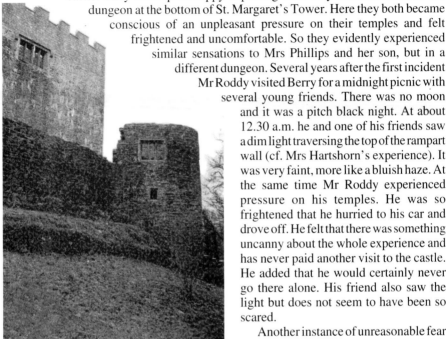

Another instance of unreasonable fear occurred at the launching of my book *Berry Pomeroy Castle* which took place at the castle on a glorious summer's day when the sun never went in for a moment. Visitors and friends were able to enjoy the beauty of their surroundings to the full and bask in the warm sunshine. Not so Chips Barber, however; he told me, some time after, that as soon as he arrived he felt gripped by a chill and oppressive feeling of fear which seemed to emanate from the castle itself. For the first time in his life he felt afraid of it, and it positively repelled him. So after he had made himself known he bought a copy of the book and hurried away. He felt he could not stay any longer—the castle literally drove him away. One wonders how many others among the hundred or so people gathered there on that bright afternoon were similarly affected.

The hauntings at Berry are not confined simply to the castle—indeed they extend to the Gatcombe valley below and even to the hill opposite. Castle Mill, mentioned in a lease of 1467, which stands in the valley just below the castle is now a farmhouse. Mr A. Ellis, who lives there, farms the surrounding hills. One spring evening he was ploughing the field adjacent to the castle. Every time he came up to the top of the hill he ran into freezing air, felt frightened for no good reason, whilst his hair stood on end and he felt shivery. As soon as the tractor took him down hill he felt perfectly normal. This happened three times after which he felt he could stand it no more and abandoned his ploughing. This phenomenon of unreasonable fear is not confined only to human beings, for some animals experience it too. Dogs, for instance, will often not so much as enter the gateway, but growl and shy away from the entrance. Mr Ellis's Alsatian bitch which lives at the Mill likes a walk as much as any dog, but if she sees that her master is going up to the castle she stays at home, for she has a profound dislike of the place. The late Mr Hamlyn Parsons used to relate how his spaniel accompanied him one day to Berry, but when it climbed the stairs up to the Rampart Walk it turned tail in fear and fled. This so interested Mr Hamlyn Parsons that he caught the dog and put it on the lead. Even so he could not succeed in dragging it towards St. Margaret's Tower. Finally he attempted to carry it in there; but it was no good the animal was scared stiff and would not be forced, coaxed, or in any way persuaded to go there.

Mr F.J. Bodley, of Shiphay,Torquay, had a similar experience with his dog. In this case the animal showed fear immediately and would not go into the Gatehouse.

Another story of animal fear was related to me by Mrs Rowden of Totnes, who for many years resided at the Castle Lodge. She related how an old couple visit the Castle every year on a certain date in September. This is because when on their honeymoon, many years ago, they went to Berry accompanied by their dog. As they walked along the Rampart Walk towards St. Margaret's Tower they suddenly walked into freezing air, whilst their hair stood on end. Though frightened they stood their ground, hoping that if they kept very still they might see something. Nothing appeared, however, but they much wondered what their dog saw, for he began to howl, and with heckles rising, turned and fled as fast as his legs would carry him. At the time when Mrs Rowden related this story there had been no repetition of their experience.

So we have sufficient testified evidence from the above reports to conclude that unreasonable fear, evidently instigated by a force which is both malignant and repelling, is the commonest of all the phenomena.

2. Records of Visible Phenomena

There are two strange things to record about the sightings of ghosts at or near the castle, the first being that whilst one may see a ghost yet his companion may not. The second is that with the notable exception of the White Lady, all the recorded sightings have been by day. Now the White Lady, according to folklore, is the ghost of Lady Margaret Pomeroy who was imprisoned by her jealous sister, Lady Eleanor, in the bottom most dungeon of St. Margaret's Tower—both sisters having fallen in love with the same man. She is seen to issue from the tower and walk along the Rampart Walk. In the folklore to see her is to die very soon, but my informants are, so far as I know, still living. So that part of the legend is manifestly untrue! She appears clad from head to foot in white—hence her name, whilst her hair streams behind her in wild disarray. I can vouch for the reliability of the witnesses of four appearances of this ghost. Chips Barber of Pinhoe, Exeter, related to me how in April, 1963, when a boy of 13, he visited the castle with

other boys. It was about 6 o'clock of a spring evening and they were playing football on the lawn before the Gatehouse. As luck would have it Chips took a mighty kick and the ball sailed right over the wall into St. Margaret's Tower. He ran to retrieve it, passing the custodian who was preparing to lock up. He could not find the ball. Guessing that it had rolled down the steps of the tower he scrambled down the broken stairway, and there on the floor of the comfortless dungeon was his ball. As he stooped to pick it up he turned round and saw a woman ascending the circular stairs. As she was above him he could only see her skirt which was long and came down to her feet. She disappeared upward and he thought nothing more about her until he got to the gate. Then he warned the custodian that there was still a visitor in the castle. But the custodian said that there was no one else there, and indeed a search proved this to be the case. Slowly it dawned on Chips that he had seen the ghost of the White Lady, who is said to haunt that tower. He remembered then that he had heard no sound of her footsteps; he described the skirt as showing no recognisable colour in the gathering twilight.

On Midsummer's Eve, 1983, along with several others, I kept watch until midnight at the castle. Just before midnight a party of young men drove up. One of them, Mr Craig Rowland, told us of their experience there at the same time the previous year. He said that they were all on the greensward before the Castle when they heard the tramping of many feet in the undergrowth behind them. This quite unnerved them because they could see in the bright moonlight that there was no one there. Then Craig Rowland saw the White Lady walking along the Rampart Wall. So scared was he that he made a dash for his car and drove off, leaving his companions to run after him. When they caught up with him they all stated that that they had never seen the White Lady: Craig, it appears was the only one who had. So in 1983, a year later, they had all come again on Midsummer's Eve hoping for a repeat performance. But in this they were disappointed.

A really frightening appearance of the White Lady took place in April, 1987. Mr Warren Hunt, of Paignton, told me afterwards of his infatuation for Berry and how he visited the woods and ruins at dead of night for months on end, hoping that he might see something. An end was put to his many vigils, however, in a very dramatic manner. He had parked his car one night at the Lodge gate and gone down to the castle. On this occasion he climbed in to the ruins and walked along the Rampart Wall as far as St. Margaret's Tower. This he descended to the bottom-most dungeon. It was a pitch black night and so almost completely dark down there. Suddenly the whole cell was illuminated by a blinding light, and there before him stood the White Lady. Warren did what was probably the best thing and ran for it. He was absolutely terrified, and tore up the stairs and out of the castle as fast as his legs would carry him. His one object was to get away at all costs, so he rushed down the steep path to the road and so back to his home in Paignton, never stopping for an instant. So great was his fear that he quite forgot his car and had to go and retrieve it next day. The shock of this occurrence was so great that he could not bring himself to speak of what had happened for at least a fortnight. Nothing will persuade him ever to visit the castle again,

Some years ago a newspaper published a vivid account of a night which a certain well known medium spent at Berry. The medium was said to have been too scared to leave her car which she had drawn up in front of the Gatehouse. Apparently it was constantly rocked to and fro by unseen forces, and she herself was subjected to a night of terror during which she saw the White Lady pacing up and down the Rampart Walk.

Another experience of the wiles of the White Lady was related to me by Mr Peter Kirk of Torquay. He and his wife visited the castle one evening at dusk and walked along the

Rampart Walk. As they approached St. Margaret's Tower Mrs Kirk said she would go no further as she felt it was spooky just there; so Mr Kirk left her to go back on her own whilst he went on to the top of the tower staircase. Here he began to feel uneasy and shivery, yet he somehow felt impelled to continue down the stairs to the bottom-most dungeon. When he finally reached this gloomy spot he actually beheld the White Lady awaiting him. He felt that somehow she had lured him there. Panic then seized him and he rushed back up the stairs and out of the castle, not stopping to explain what he had seen to his wife until they reached the tea-room. Here he was told that his experience was by no means uncommon. Neither he nor Mrs Kirk had heard anything of the hauntings prior to their visit and so his experience came as a complete shock to both of them.

The hauntings by the Blue Lady take us right back to the end of the eighteenth century, and the story now to be related is the earliest I have so far found in connection with the castle. It concerns Dr (later Sir) Walter Farquhar. He was latterly physician to King George IV, but at the time of this occurrence was practising in Torquay—a town which was just starting to grow. Quoting now from Annals of the Seymours note 98, p.443, the writer, after telling how the doctor was summoned one day from Torquay to make a professional visit to Berry Pomeroy Castle, continues as follows:

"Although a ruin, there still remained two or three rooms in which the steward resided with his wife. It was the latter who was ill. On the doctor's arrival he was asked to remain in the outer apartment while the steward went to see if his wife was prepared. This apartment was large and ill-proportioned; around ran richly carved panels of oak that age had changed to the hue of ebony. The only light in the room was admitted through the chequered panes of a gorgeously stained window, in which were emblazoned the arms of the former Lords of Berry Pomeroy. In one corner to the right of the wide fireplace was a flight of dark oaken steps, forming part of a staircase leading apparently to some chamber above. Whilst the doctor was waiting the door opened, and a richly dressed lady entered the room. The doctor thinking it was some visitor, rose and stepped forward, but the lady paid no attention to him, and hurried across the room, wringing her hands, and evidently in the greatest distress. Arriving at the foot of the stairs, she paused a moment and then hurried up them. As she reached the highest stair the light fell strongly on her features, and displayed a young and beautiful countenance, but to use the doctor's own words, 'If ever human face exhibited agony and remorse: if ever the eye, that index of the soul, portrayed anguish uncheered by hope and suffering without interval: if ever features betrayed that within the wearer's bosom there dwelt a hell, those features and that being were then present to me.'

"Almost immediately afterwards he was called to see the patient whom he found so ill that he had to give his undivided attention to her case. The next day, however, finding her much better, he enquired of the steward as to the lady he had seen, and described her appearance. The steward became greatly agitated, exclaiming repeatedly, 'my poor wife!' But eventually, becoming calmer, he told the doctor that he was now sure that she would die, and enlightened him as to the history of the apparition so far as he knew it. It appears that it was the daughter of a former baron of Berry Pomeroy, who had borne a child to her own father and strangled it in the room above. He added that he had lived in the castle for 30 years, and had never known the omen fail, and that it had last been seen the day his son was drowned. Although the doctor considered his patient much better and pronounced that all danger was over the omen had been no mistake and the poor woman died that day.

"Many years afterwards Sir Walter was called upon by a lady who came to consult him about her sister who was suffering from severe shock. She explained that during the summer she had accompanied her brother and sister to Torquay, whence they had driven over one morning to inspect the ruins of Berry Pomeroy.

"The steward they found was ill, and there was difficulty about getting the keys. She herself and her brother had therefore gone in search of them, leaving their sister in a large outer room (apparently, from her description, the same as that in which the doctor had been put). When they returned they found their sister in a terrible state of alarm and distress, declaring that she had seen an apparition (the description of which tallied exactly with that formerly seen by Sir Walter). They had endeavoured to rally her out of it by expressing their disbelief and laughing at her fear: but their sister only grew worse and her state now occasioned the greatest alarm . In reply to a question of Sir Walter's she said that the steward had died whilst they were at the castle. The doctor then said, 'Madam, I will make a point of seeing your sister immediately, but it is no delusion. This I think it most proper to state before any interview. I, myself, saw the same figure under somewhat similar circumstances, and about the same hour of the day. I should decidedly oppose any raillery or incredulity being expressed on the subject in your sister's presence.' The lady recovered and the apparition was never seen again for the old steward was the last person to inhabit the castle."

The final sentence in the above account has been proved incorrect, however, and I can give further accounts of appearances of the Blue Lady; and my next instance is from this century and is quoted from the late Elliott O'Donnell's *Screaming Skulls and other Ghost Stories*. He relates how at the International Club for Psychical Research in 1913 a Mr Taylor related a story told him by Mrs King of Torquay. She stated that her brother who was an army officer, went, whilst on leave, to see Berry Pomeroy Castle. Whilst wandering over the ruins he saw a young and beautiful girl beckoning to him from the summit of one of the lofty ivy-clad walls. She was wearing a somewhat quaint, though becoming, blue costume. He, supposing that she was afraid to move lest she should fall, hastened to find a way to reach her. Having begun to climb up to her he had almost reached her when the masonry beneath his feet gave way, and it was only by a miracle that he managed to save himself from falling headlong to a considerable depth. Clinging desperately to a narrow ledge, he was, luckily for himself, eventually seen and rescued. But on mentioning the plight of the lovely damsel he was told that there was no reason to concern himself about her—she was not of this world but the much dreaded phantom of a long defunct member of the Pomeroy family, who took a fiendish delight in luring people, especially men, to their destruction.

An account of a recent sighting of the Blue Lady was given to me by Mrs Ellis who ran the Tea Room beside the castle. She related how a little while back a clergyman, his wife and daughter visited Berry one summer's afternoon. They entered the castle beneath the Gatehouse and as they did so the daughter, who was about eighteen, suddenly cried out and then fainted. She was assisted to the nearby Tea Room where Mrs Ellis happened to be. The girl was brought round and stated that she had seen the sudden apparition of a young woman dressed in blue who had beckoned to her from the gateway. Her face was evil and this, and her sudden appearance, had caused her to faint. Mrs Ellis suggested to her that it was all her imagination and that she must have been reading about the castle and its ghosts before she came. But the father assured her that a quarter of an hour ago they had never so much as heard of Berry Pomeroy Castle. They had happened to notice the signpost and decided, on the spur of the moment, to go there.

Another sighting of the Blue Lady occurred in 1980, when Mrs Jane Everitt of Torquay visited Berry with friends. It was about 2 p.m. and they left by way of the steep path which leads to the valley below. Mrs Everitt glanced back to take a look at the buildings from below and was surprised to see a figure standing at the window of one of the rooms in the top storey at the back of the castle. The others, however, could not see it. She wondered how anyone had got up there, and then she slowly realised that there were no floors for anyone to stand on and that this must be none other than a ghost. Every time she looked back the figure was still watching them. It appeared to be a female and was clad in blue or purple.

So appearances of the Blue Lady can still be recorded in recent times. From her first recorded sighting by Sir Walter Farquhar at the end of the eighteenth century is a span of two centuries. This sad but beautiful ghost seems still to haunt the old building where she committed so horrible a crime.

The Black Hound

Some years ago, Mrs Aya Broughton, an artist of international repute, went with her husband to Berry one beautiful summer's afternoon. She wanted on that occasion to do a painting of the castle. She settled in the Courtyard whilst her husband went for a walk. No one was about and the silence was somehow uncanny. The brightness of the light, too, was unusual. She remembered this later on. In those days before the restoration there was thick ivy on the ruined walls where birds nested, and on this fine day some were even basking in the sunshine upon the ground. Suddenly the whole flock rose into the air, wheeling round and crying out in alarm. At the same moment she was conscious of the presence of a huge black hound. This dog was quite alone and paced up and down before her. It was evil, sinister and, worst of all, menacing. It came very close, but not right up to her. Being psychic, Mrs Broughton realised at once that this was no ordinary dog, but an apparition. Feeling that at all costs she must not lose her nerve, she tried to go on painting, though terribly afraid. She repeated a Buddhist prayer for use in the presence of evil spirits, 'May all beings be happy!' After what seemed an eternity the hateful thing gradually faded and then disappeared.

Her husband very soon came back from his walk saying that he didn't want to stay away too long because he had heard that the place was haunted and wondered if she was all right.

An Old Man with a Scythe

My wife used to recall visiting Berry Pomeroy on a certain occasion when a child. She was with her mother and a little friend. When they arrived there was some difficulty over getting the key, but her mother, Mrs Charlesworth, saw an old man with a scythe cutting the grass in front of the Gatehouse. 'Run along and ask that old man if he has the key', she said to my wife. But although the two children ran off in the direction indicated, they saw no one and came back again. Mrs Charlesworth said, 'Why he's just over there, can't you see him?' and thereupon went herself. She soon returned, however, saying, 'He's dressed in such strange clothes and looks quite evil. I really didn't like to speak to him.' Mrs Charlesworth was well known for her psychic powers, and in this case evidently saw the old man quite clearly, but the children could not.

Appearance of Blue Light

On Midsummer's Eve, 1983, whilst doing a ghost watch at the castle, I was seated on the Rampart Walk in front of the Guardroom door. On my left was Mr R. Daulby and on my right a medium who wishes to remain anonymous. A little before midnight I saw a faint blue light emanating from St. Margaret's Tower. I asked Mr Daulby, 'Can you see that?' but he couldn't. I repeated my question to the medium and she replied that she could. We watched whilst the light increased in intensity, and then, just like a pricked bubble, it suddenly vanished. Note that by saying to my companions 'Can you see that?', they had no means of knowing just what I had seen. But the medium said afterwards that she had seen a light and later described it just as I had seen it. It will be remembered that a similar light has already been described by both Mrs Hartshorn and Mr Roddy. In the case of the first there was also a small white cloud visible over the building. This phenomenon occurs again quite frequently in photographs.

Visible Phenomena seen near the Castle

Mr Ellis of Castle Mill has already been mentioned. He had another psychic experience one evening when milking in a building adjoining the mill. He saw what he thought to be his nephew dodging in and out among the cows and disturbing them. He shouted at him to stop it, whereupon the figure disappeared. On going back to the house he found, to his surprise, that his nephew was seated in front of the fire and had never been out at all. The figure he had seen was hooded but resembled his nephew in height and build.

Mrs Rowden, formerly of the Castle Lodge, told me that there used to be a wooden footbridge across the stream below the mill. Here many people have seen an old lady in quaint, old-fashioned garments. She was always in the centre of the bridge with a smile on her face—not in the least alarming. Unfortunately the bridge has been removed and the figure has never been seen again. Miss E. Beveridge and a friend once saw in the mill yard a dark, sullen girl squatting on the wall who glared at them with great hostility. The full story of this unpleasant encounter is related later under the heading of "Going back in Time".

Appearance of Cavalier

Mr & Mrs V. Hills of Barton Hill Road, Torquay, told me that in 1980, on the Friday before Christmas, they were both driving home from Totnes at 8.30 p.m. They had just passed Berry Pomeroy School when they saw a dim haze in front of them although the weather was clear. As they drove up the hill to the narrow bends they were both amazed to see the figure of a cavalier crossing the road in front of them. He wore a large hat with a feather, doublet and hose: his hair was in ringlets and he had a bushy moustache, curling up at the ends. She described his colouring as grey and white, but misty with dark and light tones. He crossed the road from one hedge to the other but was walking on a level higher than the road surface, i.e. on the level of the surrounding fields. He smiled at them and indicated to Mrs Hills that he was only going to the hostelry. He did not actually speak but conveyed that meaning to her, but not to Mr Hills.

Exactly two weeks later Mr Hills was driving along the same road at 4.45 p.m. and saw the cavalier again at the road junction where the sign post to the castle stands. He was coming from the castle and crossed the main road, but this time on the same level; he crossed to a gateway where there is an old right of way to the village. He gazed at Mr Hills but did not speak or smile.

3. Freezing Air

To pass from the phenomenon of visible appearances to that of freezing air is quite logical for both sensations often occur together and are not peculiar to Berry. The cold air may be also accompanied by bristling of the hair and shivers down the spine. Sometimes these symptoms precede an appearance, sometimes they come hard on its heels.

We have already mentioned freezing air in the cases of Mrs Anne Wright and her friend, of Mr R. Daulby and his medium friend and of Mr Ellis when ploughing. Later you will read of it being experienced by Mr J. Hazzard and his workmate Bernie. In addition I can mention two odd experiences where freezing air occurred: first consider what happened to Mr Bridgeman of Torquay, my postman. He is a keen photographer and one bright summer's morning took a photo of the Gatehouse. Afterwards he climbed up to the

Guardroom and as soon as he entered it he stepped into very cold air whilst his hair stood on end. At the time he did not pay much attention to it, but when the photo was developed what should it show but the figure of a man or woman wearing a white ruffle and standing at one of the Guard room windows. He then remembered how, just after taking the photo, he had experienced the freezing air and began to think how odd it was that the two things followed so quickly one after the other. The whole incident will be considered more fully under the category of Photographic Phenomena.

A Mr and Mrs Rupert Everitt of Edginswell, Torquay, also experienced cold air and shivering—not at the castle itself, but on the hillside opposite. Again their paranormal adventure will be related under categories 7 and 8.

4. Paranormal Sounds

We will consider next the category of paranormal sounds and will mention first the unexplained sounds which I and others heard when on a nocturnal vigil one summer's night. We were seated up against the Guardroom door, overlooking the Rampart walk. All was still and tranquil. We were all relaxed and cheerful—almost forgetting the purpose of our visit—when we suddenly heard the sound of something dropping in the Guardroom behind us. What it could have been I still do not know. It was not heavy enough to be described as a thud, not sharp enough to have been a piece of metal, not dull enough for wood. But it nevertheless resounded ominously in the empty chamber behind us. All within would be secure and neatly stacked just as the workmen had left it. There should have been nothing to drop—yet we had all heard that distinct and unnerving sound. What ever was it? Not long after a door slammed somewhere in the house. Strange, because there was not a breath of wind, neither was there a door anywhere which could have banged. The many doors in the castle once upon a time had long since mouldered to decay. Indeed the only doors now existing were those belonging to the workmen's huts, but these were all firmly secured each night against vandals. Nevertheless, we had all heard the sound of the slamming of a door which could not have existed, and when there was no wind strong enough to slam it even if it had!

And so we sat and pondered over the two sounds which we had heard. I do not think

The Ghosts of Berry Pomeroy Castle

any of us were quite as relaxed as we had been. And then about half an hour later I distinctly heard the latch of the Guardroom door turned—ever so gently. An unseen hand was at work. Had we stayed any longer then fear would have taken hold of us—and that is the moment to get away before anything worse takes over. I do not know if the others heard that final sound, but when I rose and suggested that we called it a day there were no dissenting voices!

Of all the sounds which surely belong to another plane of existence surely the most exciting are those of the galloping hoofbeats of the Pomeroy brothers as they spurred their chargers over the cliff to certain death. The two brothers, when besieged and driven to the point of surrender, chose to save their families and retainers from the horrors of surrender to a ruthless foe by the giving of their own lives. Dressed in armour and all the splendid accoutrements of mediaeval warfare, they mounted their chargers, galloped along the north terrace and spurred them over the brink of the precipice on which the castle stands, thus riding to a terrible death. The drama of this event was recaptured one night when Professor Raymond Cattell and his wife heard these very sounds.

In his book *Under Sail Through Red Devon* (1937) are lively and entertaining descriptions of sailing round the Devon coast and up some of the rivers. Cattell describes sailing up to Totnes and disembarking there. Mentioning Berry Pomeroy Castle he asserts that it takes a brave man to go there alone at night, to climb over the gate, enter the silent ruin and perhaps hear, as he did, the hoofbeats of the Pomeroys' horses as they charged over the precipice.

I checked this reference with Raymond Cattell, now living in Hawaii and he wrote as follows: "My wife and I were living at Dartington at the time, and since Berry was less set up with keepers and regulations then we would sometimes take a moonlight stroll there. The clearest we heard the sound of the hoofbeats was when standing on

The White Lady

the greensward just by the castle. I was describing the event to my wife, so it might have been the vividness of our imagination, but suddenly, almost as if from out the sky, we heard galloping. We thought we could even hear the clink of the horseshoes on stones. Then there was a distinct cry and what sounded like suppressed screams."

This was, to say the least, an amazing experience:it is to be noted that both heard the same sounds. The beginning of the letter suggests that they had heard the sound of galloping on previous occasions, but less clearly. It is remarkable too that after over fifty years the Professor was still prepared to stand by the story which is still quite clear in his mind. So far I have not yet met any one else who has experienced this gripping phenomenon.

The adventure of Craig Rowland and his companions on Midsummer's Eve, 1982, has already been mentioned but must be considered again under the category of paranormal sounds, because they all testified to having heard the sound of tramping feet in the undergrowth behind them. This they found most unnerving because in the bright moonlight they could see that there was no one there—yet they could hear the sounds.

Associated with the story of the Lady in Blue are the sounds of the crying baby which she is said in folklore to have been smothered. I had always tended to regard this as a legendary sound, but was suddenly made to change my mind on meeting Miss Heather Reilly of Brunswick Terrace,Torquay, on January 19th, 1985. She was at the time a nurse at Rowcroft Hospice. She said that in the autumn of 1982 she and three other girl friends decided to spend the night at the castle. It turned out to be a wild night and pouring with rain. As they drove past the castle towards the car park they were all aware that the Gatehouse was closed and the entrance blocked by a massive iron-studded gate—a portcullis no doubt. But after they had parked the car and approached the castle they were more than surprised to find that this formidable barrier had simply disappeared. Nothing barred the entrance but the usual lightly constructed slatted gate. On account of the pouring rain they were compelled to pass the night comfortless beneath the Gatehouse. At about one o'clock Miss Reilly distinctly heard the cries of a baby. This phenomenon seemed to come from the woods near the car park. The cries were intermittent and lasted

The Ghosts of Berry Pomeroy Castle

for about a quarter of an hour. An interesting point was that none of her companions heard the sound.

5. Touch

So far we have considered the categories of unreasonable fear, visible appearances, freezing air and paranormal sounds. We will consider next the risk you run when you go to Berry of being touched by an unseen hand. The phenomenon is rare and I have but one example of it.

Mrs Stella Joint of Torquay related to me how a few years previously, when in her teens, she had visited the castle at dusk one Midsummer's Eve. She and a party of young people from Paignton Parish Church had decided to go in fancy dress for the occasion. Mrs Joint and the rest of the party climbed up to the Rampart walk and continued along it in the direction of St. Margaret's Tower. They all began to clamber down inside the tower, but Mrs Joint stayed where she was, so for a few minutes she was quite alone. She then felt a hand placed upon her shoulder and a gentle shove from behind. Thinking that one of her friends had stayed behind and crept up on her, she looked round to see who it was. To her horror, there was no one there! So unnerved was she by this incident that she could not take part in the fun of the evening, neither could she bring herself to tell any of her friends what had occurred. It was only when she got home that she felt able to discuss it with her mother. They both felt it quite remarkable that for her fancy dress she went as the White Lady. We shall read what had already happened to the party on the way down the drive under category 7.

6. Photographic Failures

Blank films, camera shutters not working, misty patches, yes, and ghosts appearing where none were seen by the photographer are some of the photographic phenomena at Berry. The first three occurrences are very common indeed. My wife, for instance, once had a whole film come out blank for no good reason. A lady came up to me after a lecture which I had given at Newton Abbot and said that all the photos which she had taken on a recent film were excellent with the exception of one taken at Berry—that was a blank!

A few years ago ITV cameramen came down to take shots of the castle by night. On the first night all their cameras jammed and they just could not get the shutters working. The next night they came again with cameras checked and working perfectly. But yet again the castle got the better of them and everything jammed. As to what happened on the third night, read section 8.

A certain Mr Bullocke attended a lecture of mine at Paignton. I told this story to the audience and afterwards he said to me, 'I'm in my eighties now, but in the 1920s I well remember the Stoll Picture Co., who were well known at the time, sending cameramen to the castle and exactly the same thing happened to them, for all their cameras jammed.' That takes us back over 60 years with the same phenomena occurring.

Take next the case of Mrs May of Saltash. She is a member of the Saltash and District Cine Group. She and a Mr Ronald Allen, also a member, went to the castle on April 16th, 1983. Their idea was to get useful ideas for a feature film. They arrived at about 11.30 on a rather misty morning, and decided to work separately for an hour. After about half an hour she came across Mr Allen who said his camera was not working in spite of being carefully checked the previous evening. But nothing would register now—the iris from the lens had gone on strike. Back at the car the camera was rechecked and everything should have been plain sailing: but on returning to the castle again it would not work. It was therefore thrown into the boot in disgust. After lunch Mrs May's camera, described as "very basic" was used with success. Then they thought they would give Mr Allen's camera one more chance. It worked like a charm! They used up some 30 feet of film. It was sent off to "Pernchrome Service", the London Processors. But judge of their surprise when they received the following from "Pernchrome": 'We are extremely sorry to advise you ... a most unfortunate accident to your film...'! Can it really be that the power of the Berry Pomeroy hauntings can exert their influence so far? But it would appear that they can, and in category 14 a further example is given.

Then there is the case of Mr R. Daulby. He is an expert photographer and visited the castle with me in May, 1983. We went down to the valley below as he wished to photograph the ruins from there. We realised that as foliage was beginning to appear on the trees it would be the next December before the opportunity would present itself again. A very sophisticated camera was used and the light was reasonably good and clear. But the prints were misty and, for no good reason, unsatisfactory. Further photos were taken at the same time inside St. Margaret's Tower. Here two shots were complete blanks.

I will now introduce Mr Bridgeman who has already been mentioned under category 4. Before ascending to the Guardroom he had taken a photo of the Gatehouse in the bright morning sunlight. When printed this showed the face of a man or woman (it is hard to say which) looking out of the first storey window of the right hand tower. The figure is wearing a large white ruffle, so typical of the Elizabethan period. This came as a complete surprise to Mr Bridgeman who did not see this apparition when taking the photo. Only the camera saw that. Another curious result was that although the sun was shining brightly at the time, the facade of the house has come out very dark—almost black. A later photo was taken some minutes after and from a slightly different angle. Everything here appears normal and there is no signs of the apparition.

Mr and Mrs Ellis have in their possession an old but very clear photo of the façade of the house. Gazing out of one of the first floor windows is a man who by his dress would appear to belong to the Stuart period. Just the head and shoulders are visible. Nothing is known of the origin of this photo. Unfortunately it is more than possible that it is a deliberate fake. Indeed, many of the snapshots of "ghosts" which I have seen are so crude and stupid that they cannot for a moment be taken seriously. Mr Bridgeman's is beyond doubt the most convincing ghost photograph which I have so far seen.

7. Inexplicable Engine Failures

A really interesting case of engine failure was related to me by Mr and Mrs Rupert Everitt of Edginswell, Torquay. They said that during the hay harvest of 1981 they were working in the field immediately opposite the castle, but on the other side of the valley. They were working on late one evening as rain was expected. It was quite dark as they took the final load from the field. In the gateway the tractor's engine suddenly failed, and at the same time the lights went off. Mr Everitt was conscious at the same time of being suddenly in freezing air and feeling shivery. Then after a few moments the lights came on again, quite of their own accord and the engine also came to life. The whole chain of strange events could only have taken a few seconds at most and Mr Everitt's foot never left the accelerator. The time was just on midnight!

I have discussed this occurrence with motor mechanics and all agreed that with a diesel engine there is no normal explanation of the phenomenon. Unlike a car, lights and engine are independent. So the failure of both lights and engine had no connection with each other—or ought not to have done. More remarkable still, of course, was the way the engine restarted of its own accord, evidently through the agency of an unseen power. And the lights also came on quite independently. Altogether the Everitts were given a free demonstration of the work of an occult force.

The Midsummer Eve's frolics of the party from Paignton have already been alluded to under Category 5. The arrival by car of Mrs Joint and her party must now be considered.

The Ghosts of Berry Pomeroy Castle

It will be recalled that she in her fancy dress represented the White Lady. Just as the party swung into the drive they were discussing the White Lady and saying that not for a moment did they believe such rubbish. Whereupon at that very moment the engine broke down and nothing would persuade it to start up again. After much time spent in fruitless attempts they all had to help push the car back to the nearest passing place where it was abandoned for the night and towed away in disgrace next day.

8. Failure of Lighting

Perhaps rather akin to the foregoing category are the cases of inexplicable failure of lighting. It seems at Berry that the same hostile power which can stop engines and cameras from working can also disrupt lighting. It has been mentioned in Category 6 above how ITV cameramen came to the castle and were unable to photograph there owing to the jamming of their cameras. Their third night was no more successful because the floodlighting would not function. Although their batteries were new and had been thoroughly tested, nothing could be got out of them. Once more the team had to abandon their project.

The second and more recent case was the failure of the lights on Mr Everitt's tractor which has just been discussed under 7 above.

9. Possession by Another Entity

This very unpleasant phenomenon was experienced by Mr Moore of Pyworthy. He wrote to me as follows:

"About eighteen years ago myself and our two children visited Berry Pomeroy Castle while staying in the Torbay area. Our children were then aged about eight and five years. As soon as I walked through the castle gate I had an overpowering feeling of fear, not for myself but for the children, and I felt I had to keep them near me all the time. My wife noticed this and pointed out that I was being a bit silly as they couldn't come to any harm and they both wanted to run about and explore. I had to force myself to accept this and allow them to do so.

"I then went by myself and sat on a large stone on the lawn. The sensations I experienced

while sitting there were dreadful and so vivid, I can remember them clearly as I write this. It was as if I were another person who had had some dreadful experience, and I was full of despair and desolation. I can't remember how long I sat on the stone, but my wife saw something was wrong and came over to me and asked if I was feeling ill. She suggested that we had a cup of tea at a stall outside the gate. As soon as I walked out of the gate the feeling left me and I felt perfectly well. This experience was so upsetting at the time that I vowed I would never go inside the gate again. I would also point out at the time of my visit I had not heard or read anything about the castle or its history, so could not have been influenced in any way."

Mr Moore's urge to protect his children against a malignant power was shared by a friend of mine, Mrs Ali Khan, of Totnes—in fact their experience might almost constitute yet another category. Mrs Ali Khan related to me in 1985, how she had once visited the castle in the company of a young couple. Whilst they went to look at the ruins she remained in the car to mind their baby. As soon as she was left alone fear for the child's safety suddenly gripped her. She felt that she must protect it at all costs against an evil power. She was very relieved when the parents returned and they were able to drive away. Not until they were clear of the woods, however, did she feel at ease again.

10. Going back in time

Of all the phenomena mentioned so far, that of going back in time and, as it were, looking through a window onto the past is perhaps the most exciting, although those taking part probably felt completely bewildered at the time and not a little frightened. This is what happened to Miss E. Beveridge who visited the Castle Mill. Out for a late afternoon run in the car, with a South African friend who was staying with her, out of mere curiosity, they turned down a totally unfamiliar lane. Half a mile or so along the lane her friend's easy flow of chatter died away and an uncomfortable silence fell over them. On comparing notes afterwards it seemed that they had both simultaneously become aware of something strange and oddly disturbing in the atmosphere; then she was struck by something unusual in their immediate surroundings which she could not at first identify. She puzzled over it for a moment before she realised that the fowls scratching in a sloping field beside the track were of a breed she had never before encountered, scraggy, long-legged creatures, and in lieu of ordinary chicken houses were rough shelters of turves and branches, while certain domes of plaited straw like old-

The Ghosts of Berry Pomeroy Castle

fashioned bee-skeps apparently housed a few broody hens sitting on their eggs.

It was a perfect afternoon in May, no breath of air stirred, sunlight lay warm and golden over everything; conditions could hardly have been less sinister, and yet there was something very eerie in the atmosphere. The silence was profound, uncannily so, for the environs of a mill even so remote as this. Suddenly they rounded a corner and found themselves in a tiny farm-yard, the house to one side, some ramshackle sheds on the other and before them a swiftly flowing stream. The millhouse was small, low, and indescribably shabby, with small, deepset windows overhung with ragged thatch. The only living creature, apart from some ducks dabbling on the edge of the water, was a little girl of eleven or twelve who was sitting on a low wall which partly enclosed the yard next to the pool or stream—dirty and unkempt, with swarthy skin and coarse black hair which looked as if it had never known a brush or comb, and smouldering black eyes which were fixed on them with an unwinking stare of such intense malignity that they felt themselves more than ever intruders where they had no right to be. Her dress looked like nothing on earth but a filthy sack with holes cut in it for head and arms, and a piece of rope loosely tied about the waist. She was drawn up so that the soles of her feet were pressed vertically against the wall. Without moving a muscle she crouched there, glaring at them in a deadly silence that could be felt.

Miss Beveridge said, "Normally we should have called a greeting and asked the name of the place, but neither of us had the nerve to break the uncanny silence, seething as it was with almost murderous hostility, 'I don't like this,' Hilda muttered, starting to reverse the car in a nervous haste quite unlike her usual placidity. 'Let's get out of it as quick as we can!' Somehow she managed to turn the car in the tiny yard and we shot off down the way we had come, followed to the last by that glare of hatred which would have struck us dead if looks could kill! Neither of us spoke a word until we had passed the point in the lane at which we had first fallen silent, then we each drew a breath of relief."

They both felt like they'd strayed into something, some place or time, right out of this day and age. They decided the place was indeed there, but were they themselves there — then, now or ever? They felt like it was they that were the ghosts—on a different plane of existence.

Although shaken by the experience, Miss Beveridge had an irresistible urge to go back and have another look so, a fortnight later, without mentioning the previous visit, she took her cousin, who was visiting, out for an evening stroll. They turned without remark down the lane which led

to what she shall always think of as the Haunted Mill when, at precisely the same spot where the atmosphere had changed before, her cousin, Katie, suddenly halted and announced that she was not going any farther—she was not tired, she just didn't feel like going on. She knew there was a mill or something along there but she preferred to wait on the flowery bank beside the track.

Once more it was a perfect evening, warm and still, but there was a subtle change. The air was full of the normal sounds incidental to a farm. Cows were lowing, dogs barking— a man was whistling as he crossed a field, carrying a couple of buckets, a sheep dog trotting at his heels. The strange fowls and their rude shelter had vanished, and in their place were wooden hen houses of the usual type, while White Leghorns, Buff Orpingtons and Rhode Island Whites lined up at the hoppers for their ration of corn. The millhouse had been completely re-thatched, the roof appeared much higher, too, to provide a second storey where there could have been nothing but a loft before. The windows seemed larger, the leaded panes twinkled in the evening sunlight where before there had been gaping holes, innocent of glass. A new wing had been added, and a porch overgrown with honeysuckle or some other creeper that sprouted before the door—all in a couple of weeks! There was no dark malevolent little damsel crouching on the wall, the atmosphere was normal and serene.

When she got back to where her cousin was sitting, Katie instantly scrambled to her feet with an expression of relief, exclaiming that she'd had a horrid feeling that she might

never return; she had sensed something strange about the place, and admitted to simply not having had the courage to go on!

It is interesting to note that in these experiences all three visitors experienced the phenomenon of going back in time, the last companion evidently to a lesser degree. We must also list Mr Moore, mentioned in 9 above, in the present category, for as well as being taken over by another entity, his experience was certainly not concerned with those moments of time when he was actually at the castle, but with some other period, maybe centuries ago—he just didn't know.

In the summer of 1982 Mr and and Mrs Hills of Torquay went with their son, aged ten, on a helicopter trip from the Aircraft Museum which was then at Barton Pines. Theirs was a morning flight and it took place on a bright, sunny day. Owing to the large numbers wanting to go up they could not all go on the same flight, so Mr Hills went on his own. The trips only lasted for a short while and they just about had time to do a circuit round Torbay and Totnes, but they all agreed that they had had a good view of the castle. On discussing afterwards what they had seen of it they had all noticed that there was no scaffolding to be seen, whereas at that time the walls were surrounded by it. They had also seen turrets and pinnacles which have long since vanished and also pitched roofs which of course do not exist either, but most interesting of all smoke was coming from the chimneys. Young Hills had never actually been to the castle, but he agreed with his parents as to what they had all seen.

Later they went to the castle to see if by any chance fires had been lit for some purpose or other, but this was not the case. The usual roofless ruin greeted them and it was still surrounded by scaffolding. So all three of them appear to have gone back in time and, for a brief moment, had seen the castle as it once was.

11. Sudden Physical Disability

Feeling suddenly unwell and being affected by a feeling of weakness is yet another phenomenon which seems to be peculiar to Berry. The following illustrations are typical: In September, 1984, Mrs Ellaline Jerrard of Cleveland Road, Torquay, visited the castle with me. We were in the Guardroom inspecting the recently restored fresco when Mrs Jerrard was suddenly affected by strange sensations and felt that all her strength had been drained away, whilst she had very little control of her limbs. She found it most difficult to walk, was unsteady on her feet and felt pins and needles in her legs and back. After a few moments the sensations passed but the experience left her afraid of some unseen power which had affected her. She felt reluctant to visit Berry again whereas formerly she had always been delighted to go there. I felt nothing on that occasion, but Mr Jack Hazzard confessed that some while back he had experienced the same loss of power in his limbs and had fallen off a ladder as a result. My own encounter with this power had occurred in the same month when I did a ghost watch with Dr and Mrs Cooper and Mr Hazzard. At about one a.m., just before going home, we decided to walk all round the ruins. Like Mrs Jerrard, as soon as we got on the move I felt weak in the legs and quite lightheaded. I dismissed the sensation at the time as being due to tiredness, but now I wonder whether I too, was not subject to yet another occult power.

12. Shadows

To see the shadows of unseen objects is by no means uncommon in haunted buildings. At Berry, so far, only one example has been recorded. I cannot help feeling, however, that the phenomenon must be more common than we think—it is just not observed because visitors are busy concentrating their attention on the buildings and so may miss the shadows which make but momentary appearances. In 1981/2 Mr Hazzard and his workmate Bernie were in the old Great Hall of the Pomeroys. Just beyond the two service doors on the inner side, they both saw the shadow of a dog. It was about two feet in height. They both instinctively stooped to touch it, then suddenly realised that it had no substance and was but a shadow. It was there only for a second or two and then vanished.

13. Odours

Mr J. Hazzard testified that one day he and Bernie were on ladders working on a wall of the kitchen in the Seymour wing. They were talking of ghosts and Bernie was scoffing at the existence of the White Lady, whereupon they both noted that the temperature had suddenly dropped and that they were in air which was positively icy. Their hair stood on end and they began to shiver. This sensation soon passed to be followed by an odour of sweet perfume as if a woman had passed by.

14. An Outward-going Power

Lastly it must be recorded that there is apparently a strong outward-going power which emanates from the castle. This varies considerably, for it may be that one becomes "possessed" by the building itself and the desire to visit it on every possible occasion, or it may be that one feels the urge to do something in connection with the castle. In one extreme case it has resulted in someone living at a distance writing a lyric about the castle which she had never seen and of whose existence she was quite unaware. One day, quite out of the blue, I had a tape sent to me from Miss Rebecca Ramsden of whom I had never even heard. She told me that a few years ago she had written a lyric which was quite out of her usual style of writing. The music, strangely, was mediaeval in conception and style whilst the words were sad and melancholy.

But all became clear one day not long after when she and her parents visited Berry Pomeroy Castle for the first time. As soon as she saw it she realised that this was the place which had inspired the lyric, although at the time she wrote it she had never even heard of the castle. A further surprise was in store, for when she read my book she found that the words fitted the legend of the two sisters, portraying the grief of the one who had imprisoned the other, thereby causing her death—'Cynthia' being the jealous Lady Eleanor said to have starved her twin sister to death in St. Margaret's Tower. The words of Rebecca Ramsden's lyric are:

Cynthia's Twin

Winter is passing—spring will soon be here;
The children will play in the meadow without fear.
From a splendid sky the larks will sing
For the death of Cynthia's beautiful twin.
Her favourite roses scatter the ground
The ring that he gave her will never be found,
And the beautiful twin who will not recover
Lies in the arms of her loving mother.
Cynthia dreams in her dangerous sleep
The arms of the dead caress her to keep
The flaxen hair, the eyes that stare
Are the eyes of Cynthia's beautiful twin.
'Give me the ring that he gave me to wear
So am I wed in my eternal sleep.
Your jealous fingers bruise my skin,
Do you not love your beautiful twin?'

Chorus:

Sitting in crushed taffeta, So beautiful, but sad.
Cynthia then says, 'I am so at rest,
Soon we will be together for ever.'

So in this case the power which seems to emanate from the castle inspired someone to write both words and music which somehow belonged to Berry and its occult atmosphere. This would seem to be yet another case of the castle's occult power actually reaching someone far away. Here one can pause and compare this phenomenon with the one already related which concerned the inexplicable damaging of the film which was being processed in London.

In my own case I can testify to being completely "taken over" by the castle's influence after my very first visit when a little boy of eight. I simply could not get it out of my mind. Scarcely a day went by without my thinking of it. I don't think for the next 50 years that I ever got the place out of my system, but it all seemed to end by my writing the book *Berry Pomeroy Castle*. Having in that way done something, as it were, for the castle I felt no longer "possessed" by its spell, although I must admit that it does not take much to revive another flash of interest—the present little book, for instance.

This spell is felt by many. It is all the more odd when you consider how insignificant this building is among the castles of England. It is neither stately nor majestic and has never had any strategic importance. Its size is negligible and yet it has this

The Ghosts of Berry Pomeroy Castle

incomprehensible power to enthral.

In October 1989 I was with Mrs Ellis of Castle Mill, Berry Pomeroy, discussing this strange phenomenon of the castle's out-going power. She recalled how many years previously a psychiatrist at one of the universities told her that he had had a patient who, when under hypnosis, did nothing but talk of Berry Pomeroy Castle. The odd thing was that the patient, when in a normal condition, knew nothing at all about the castle, had never been there or read a word about it.

Isabelle

Of all the stories connected with Berry Pomeroy Castle, Bob Daulby's encounter with Isabelle is the most gripping. It stands apart from the psychic experiences so far recorded and is in a class quite by itself. Furthermore it demonstrates once again the long range power which the castle seems able to exert over those living at a distance. If anyone is inclined to doubt the veracity of the story which Bob tells they should have seen the distraught condition in which he and his wife arrived one afternoon on my doorstep to tell me of their bizarre experience. They were both still trembling with fear as a result of the traumatic night through which they had both passed. At the time of the experience Bob and I had known one another for only a few months. We had visited Berry together and he had been surprised by the phenomenon of photographic failures which were quite unaccountable, but no more.

I met Bob, Jack Hazzard, Elaine (a psychic), Peter Underwood and various others for a ghost watch on Midsummer's Eve, the night of the approaching Summer Solstice, June 23rd, 1983. When by 12.20 a.m. nothing had occurred, most of us left leaving Bob, Elaine and two others who had turned up on a motor bike, to continue the vigil. After everyone had left, Elaine and Bob decided to stay where they were, but the other couple went and sat in the dungeon at the bottom of St. Margaret's Tower. Time passed. Bob continues:

"At 2.50 a.m. Elaine and I were enjoying a peaceful night. There was not a sound coming from the young couple in the dungeon. I had bent down to pour myself out some hot soup, when suddenly and without warning the hair on the back of my neck stood on end and I was gripped with a fear I had never before experienced. I can safely say I was terrified; and what made matters worse was the fact that I could neither see nor feel any reason to be so afraid.

"I turned immediately towards Elaine and tried to utter some sound to tell her what I was feeling, but I noticed at once that her face was contorted in such a way as to reflect my own feelings. She was transfixed as she pointed in silent terror and stared at the top of the stairhead. I had never seen such fear on another's face before. It was at this point that I noticed that my face also ached from yearning to release a scream. Two, maybe three seconds later, an unbelievable sound poured from the castle's depths. The girl who had been sitting all this time in the dungeon added to my own terror by screaming at such a pitch that I thought that the very castle itself was screaming. Suddenly on a warm summer's night in the heart of Devon madness reigned.

"No one can imagine the utter terror that we all felt unless they had been there in person. I have to say at this point that I had had much experience in hauntings before this watch, but I never expected anything like this. Whatever this power was it had us all in such a grip of fear that we all felt doomed to an unimaginable fate. It was a force much greater than I had ever experienced before. At last I managed to control my emotions and come to grips with the situation, but it must be said that this took a great deal of effort. As soon as we could utter a word of rational conversation we decided there and then to leave the castle to its own destiny and interfere no longer. But it was as if the entity— whatever it was—followed us out of the grounds and none of us felt completely free until we had passed the Lodge. It was one of the longest walks of our lives."

It was not until three days had elapsed that Elaine could bring herself to describe what she saw. All she was able to discern, using her clairvoyant talent, was a black cloud—a large black cloud, but within this cloud there seemed to be embodied everything evil in this world. She had decided that never again would she so much as pass by the castle—let alone enter it ... But Bob was not satisfied ... Following this night he sat within the castle's walls on another seventeen occasions in all—eleven through the night and six through the day—but there was no repetition of the events of the night of June 23rd.

Since no further events took place at Berry he decided that this would be a good time to take a close look at a tool that has been used since prehistoric times—ouija boards. Having discovered on two occasions that his board worked well he was shaken when, on the third occasion, the glass moved erratically and speedily round the board as if, whoever it was, was in a state of panic. After some moments he ordered it to stop and give a name. The glass slowed down momentarily to spell 'Isabelle'.

Elaine, who was also present, suddenly put her hand to her mouth. As she did so the glass began to move swiftly, covering the whole board—in what seemed an uncontrollable manner. With a shocked expression, she asked whether it was the same person she had felt at Berry Pomeroy. As the question was asked the glass stopped moving for a moment and then, in answer, sped round the board coming to a dead stop on the word 'YES'. This was followed by more speeding round the board in such a way as to make them all panic a little. The room that night was absolutely electric. Trying to bring reason to the rising panic Bob posed the question "How old are you?" and received the answer 'Nine.'

A few moments later Elaine screamed. She took her finger off the glass and was visibly shocked. When asked what the matter was she replied, "I've just seen her! She's horrible! She's horrible! I saw just her head poking out of the top of the table. I couldn't see her body—just her head. She was looking up at me and grinning. She's horrible!—I'm not staying here!" After that nothing could make her stay, and she left the house, slamming the door behind her.

They put the board away as Anne (Bob's wife) decided that she, too, would call it a day, and she retired for the night. Some of their friends had left, leaving himself and two others who could not face going out into the night. Then Elaine knocked on the door and asked to stay after all as she couldn't go down the street.

An hour or so passed in relative quiet, when the silence was suddenly broken by a scream from Anne. Bob rushed upstairs not knowing what he expected to see, but he certainly did not expect to see Anne huddled in a ball and buried under the quilt. She had wrapped herself so tightly in it that it took some time before he could get her to release her grip. Some moments passed and eventually she was able to tell how, just as she was dropping off to sleep, she felt someone sitting on the back of her legs. Thinking it was Bob messing about, she told him to get off, and when the weight stayed there she got angry. But it wasn't Bob ... it was Isabelle! Anne said, "She was sitting on my legs, and when she turned to look at me and met my eyes she grinned at me—a really evil grin. Her eyes looked dead, and that grin! There was no humour in it! and I knew she wanted to harm me. She wanted to harm everyone in the house in any way she could. She's evil!"

At that moment Elaine screamed from downstairs. Bob rushed downstairs to be greeted by three very pallid faces. Elaine said, "She's there Bob, sitting in that chair, laughing at us. Can't you see her? She's evil! Look at her!" Bob looked but could see nothing at all. Elaine continued, "She's still sitting there and she's laughing at you now." He plucked up courage and sat in the chair that Isabelle was sitting in to face three very frightened people indeed. He knew he couldn't let her rule their fear like this and that if

The Ghosts of Berry Pomeroy Castle

Isabelle were there, and there was no reason to believe that she wasn't, then she would sense his own true feelings, for he was terrified himself. Then Elaine called out that Isabelle was running out of the room again, going up to Anne! He ran upstairs and called to her to sit in the chair that he sat in and not to move. Bob continues:

"I must explain that ever since Isabelle appeared, the house had gone abnormally cold and we could not get it warm. The whole night was to be taken up with Isabelle moving from one person to another. She had a thoroughly good time frightening us until we were all in a state of exhaustion. But with the cool dawn there appeared to be a respite. It was as if the daylight and the warmth of the sun had chased her away. Our friends felt able to leave and go home to bed. Later in the afternoon just as we were thinking it was all over Isabelle returned with a vengeance! Elaine, who lived only four doors away, dashed up to our house and told us that Isabelle had been rushing up and tapping her on the back! She had stood as much of it as she could. Isabelle had followed her to our house, and there she was back again with us all! This time I could feel her myself. Apparently she must have been very strong to allow herself to be felt by a non-psychic like myself. I had not known what fear was until I felt that first 'touch', for want of a better word. Both Anne and Elaine had my full sympathy, since neither had any protection against this monstrous little girl.

"For the following three days things were very much the same as the previous one. The nights were terrifying and the days not much better. We were at our wits end. I telephoned the friends who had been with us on the first night, but none had been bothered by Isabelle again. We all thought that it would never end and sorely wished that we had never been to Berry Pomeroy. Finally on the third night I had a very strange dream. Suffice it to say that on waking I knew that I had Isabelle beaten. I knew that she could not possibly bother me again, and knowing this made me able to convince both Anne and Elaine to fear her no longer. In a very short time I related my dream to them both, and its meaning to me, and convinced them too."

That night Bob brought out the ouija board again, knowing that Isabelle would talk. On this occasion there were just the three of them, Elaine, Anne and himself. The glass did not move at his first three attempts at trying to make contact, but the fourth attempt brought Isabelle to the board. He told her he was no longer frightened of her, she was just a little girl, that it wasn't her they disliked but the frightening things she did. Over the following nine months, through the ouija board, they were able to glean a great deal of information about the way of life that Isabelle led and the real reasons why she had chosen their house as opposed to the homes of others who had visited the castle, and of course about her death. Her story follows:

In a year unspecified she had been born to a Pomeroy. Isabelle knew him only as 'Sire'. She was rarely allowed to see him since she was born a bastard and was naturally an embarrassment. But she was not so much of an embarrassment that she had to be hidden away in another part of the country. She lived her entire existence within the stone walls of Berry Pomeroy. She was not given the freedom of the whole building; only certain parts were open to her, but the freedom was usually curtailed whenever guests appeared. She could name no guests, neither could she name her father or mother nor could she name her one friend within those walls.

Isabelle said she was a 'Pomeroy pet' in that she had always been dressed in the very best finery of the day and respected to a certain degree by all the servants. After all, a Pomeroy in part was better then no Pomeroy at all. This alone raised her above servitude. She was carried to bed each night by a servant, and her room in any season was always warm and aired, whilst fresh linen was put on the bed. She never knew what it was to be soiled and royalty could not have been treated better. She ate the very best in the way of food, usually rabbit, venison and sometimes beef or pork. She drank the very best wines. Port was always imported, but she had no idea where it came from and had never heard of Portugal or France. She could tell a bad wine from a good one.

One evening 'Sire' and a few friends returned from a successful day's hunting. They were boisterous and full of stories of the bravery of their horses and the various kills they had made that day. They made their way to the kitchen where they all began to gorge themselves on the ample cooked meats and cheeses, but especially the wines. Here they had a veritable orgy as bottle succeeded bottle. It was indeed a gentlemen's party! Suddenly one of them caught sight of a very attractive maid who had been waiting on them and they proceeded to draw her on to the table, stripping her of her clothes and ignoring her terrified screams. One man was about to rape her there and then, when Isabelle, thinking that they were still out hunting, entered the room.

One cannot imagine the effect this had on such an innocent, for the victim was her mother. She was surrounded by drunks, who were laughing and egging one another on, but all Isabelle could hear were the screams of her terrified mother. Instantly, with no thought for herself, she ran into the centre of the group and tugged as hard as she could on her mother's arm, trying to free her from a terror which she herself could not understand. 'Sire' and his friends did not notice at first what this girl was doing, nor the tears which streamed down her face, nor could they have known the damage done to her soul, her mind and heart. One of the men (not seen by Isabelle before) merely glanced at the girl, then took a swipe at her, sending her flying off her feet. She landed head first on the stone floor and died instantly. So she died whilst trying to save her mother.

She did not know at first that she was dead. All she knew, as she regained her feet, was that she had to try again. So she made her way to the centre of the group once more. It seemed much easier than before and she made another attempt to pull her mother's arm: but something was wrong—very wrong. Her hands kept going through her mother's hands and body. Trying to ignore her initial confusion she made many attempts, but all to no avail. That day a nine year old girl saw her mother raped repeatedly in an indescribable manner, whilst slowly it dawned on this intelligent girl that she herself had been killed. She was dead!

For over five hundred years the horrors of that night were to plague her very being. The torture of mental confusion caused Isabelle to remain earth-bound and in a negative state. She wandered the castle and the surrounding area but never outside its perimeter. During this time she saw the last of the Pomeroys leave the castle and the advent and final departure of the Seymours. But of more importance to her was the eventual opening of the castle to visitors. During the lives of members of the two great families who lived at the castle there must have been a number of sensitives, yet they were never to match the number that eventually visited the castle when once the general public were admitted. Time itself gave Isabelle great strength and she grew quite rapidly, not in a physical sense, but in a mental one, and not in an academic sense. Her powers grew as she discovered that the only way that she could gain any attention at all was to frighten anyone with any form of psychic ability. It mattered not whether they were conscious of it or not. There were many to choose from. When the castle was deserted and began to lose its initial lustre it was from time to time used for all kinds of strange practices. Strange in that local covens thought it a good site: young and rowdy people thought it a good site and various other classes with no good intent in mind thought it a good site, also; very few good, upright or innocent people would actually remain at the castle all night. So this was Isabelle's playground and her only form of contact with the 'outside' world. However, after nine

The Ghosts of Berry Pomeroy Castle

months of living within a normal family environment, she was introduced to a greater, stronger and more positive spirit from higher realms, and slowly was led away. She was reunited with her mother and is growing very well in a warm and loving atmosphere. She is free from Berry Pomeroy and free from its memory.

Bob says that Isabelle was not the only entity there in the negative state of being earthbound, for apparently there was something far stronger at the castle than Isabelle. Anne and he and another area investigator from ASSAP used the ouija board one night. They spoke to an entity who purported to be the 'White Lady' but he could not repeat her narrative as her language was among the foulest he had ever heard. She too, was not the only 'other' one.

Initially Bob had informed me that after Isabelle there were no others to be found at Berry, but then reports continued to reach him of strange events still taking place—long after Isabelle had left and moved on. Over a period of three years following her case he discovered that there were another twenty-six negative spirits in and around the castle— he considered Berry Pomeroy to be literally infested with evil!

Bob's theory as to why it was that certain things were felt, seen or experienced at some times and not others is because there are other sites all over the country which these spirits used to visit en masse, and Berry was only one on the list of places visited and haunted. But having said that, Berry happened to be the strongest point. He feels that it all has a great deal to do with more than one ley line which crosses the actual site.

Bob concludes: "Eventually all earthbound spirits from the castle were moved by us, but only for the moment. You see, because it is not unlike a flame to a moth, the castle will always attract those from the lower plane, and, I feel, even long after the castle has ceased to exist this site, in particular, will remain what it is. And here I strongly advise against the use of ouija boards, for one never knows what may follow one home! From personal experience I can say that spirits from Berry must be guarded against. In any event it is better not to use contact with those that have passed on, unless under controlled or supervised situations and conditions. One may well ask whether Isabelle ever really did exist—certainly there is no written record of her, and no mention of a Pomeroy bastard, male or female—but would there be? However I feel sure that one day, maybe long after my sojourn here, Berry will change. As it changes, so the grounds around it will change— into what? One can only guess: but as the soil is turned, and from deep in the ground, a skeleton of a young girl of eight or nine will be discovered. 'Who,' they will then ask, 'was this young girl?' "

Conclusion

So what conclusions may be drawn from the evidence provided? Certainly when so many responsible folk have testified to so many occult experiences the mass of evidence provided cannot be lightly dismissed. In a few cases, certainly, the people concerned did know of the castle's reputation before they went there: but in the bulk of the cases this simply was not so their experiences came to them out of the blue as a complete shock which makes them all the more convincing.

The intriguing variety of the phenomena is nothing short of amazing. Just consider them for a moment—the expected visible ghost is not to the fore, and instead we have unreasonable fear, unexplained sounds, cold air, physical disability, scents, shadows, camera and electrical failures, a force that can be felt, possession by another entity, seeing back in time and going back as well. Most curious of all is the long range power which grips certain people and causes them to react, even at a distance. Lastly, and in a class quite by itself comes the story of Isabelle and her manifestation four or five miles away from the castle.

It is a mixed bag, indeed, and one wonders whether there is another haunted spot anywhere which has produced such a variety of psychic experiences. A question which always puzzles me is this—are the ghosts at the castle putting on a show now at this very moment, just for sheer *joie de vivre* as it were? Is the White Lady pacing up and down the Rampart Walk and is there a sound of galloping hooves as the Pomeroy brothers urge their steeds over the dread abyss? Or must there always be people present to trigger off phenomena? If so, then it would appear to be an outgoing power from ourselves which produces psychic activities—rather like striking a match. Psychic people, particularly mediums, would seem to have the best chance of seeing and feeling things which are paranormal. Yet in many of the stories in the book it is sometimes the sceptic who has the interesting experience. It has been noted that a ghost watch at night consisting of two or three kindred spirits may result in a peaceful occasion: but just try introducing a jittery stranger to the party and an uneasy watch for all may result.

It is only natural, yet unfortunate, that those who have been most deeply frightened at Berry are quite determined never to go there again, for they have sensed the danger of confronting the very strong evil force which sometimes descends on this uncanny building like a dark cloud. Therefore we cannot watch with them again as we would like to do. This evil force is perceived by some at once and they get away as quickly as may be, but with others (as in the case of Bob Daulby and Elaine) it takes some time to penetrate.

It always seems to me that the natural position of the castle should be taken into account along with the hauntings . The intersection of ley lines here should certainly be considered, also the strange amphitheatre of high hills which surround the ruins in a semicircle.

Could it be that we have here a unique site where in prehistoric times long forgotten rituals were enacted? The dramatic position of the site is of course best seen in winter when foliage does not obscure the height of the impressive hills.

In conclusion it can be said that Berry Pomeroy Castle poses some tantalising problems to the explorer of the occult and will continue to do so, I predict, for many years to come. Indeed "There are more things in heaven and earth, Horatio, than are dreamt of in your philosophy."

The Ghosts of Berry Pomeroy Castle